Dry Lake

poems

Shelly Norris

Published by:
Powder River Publishing LLC
1014 Black Mountain Road
Thermopolis, Wyoming 82443

Interleaf Photo by Rob Koelling
Dedication Photos from Author's Collection
Author Photo by Lacey F. Bell

In *Dry Lake* Shelly Norris speaks in the language of geology, landscapes, and nature. This is not merely a conceit or even a poetic memoir. Rather, Norris creates a poetic alchemy, matching the interior with the exterior, the soul with its worldly environs. From leaves quivering at the top of Aspens to the green-black depths of icy lakes, Norris enters the natural world to meditate on self, on family history, on trauma, on existence. She writes, *Here we are again, a shallow/brooding inactive caldera,* from which she charts the expansiveness of a soul, as well as her own resilience, across time and multiple states: Missouri, the Dakota Badlands, Wyoming. These poems, born of the heartland, are perfumed with wild prairie roses, celebrate pioneer and cowboy heritage, chronicle plagues of locusts, backbreaking work, and even a bit of old-time religion. Norris captures a world that seems stark only to those who don't look carefully. She explores the ways nature strips us of affectations, boils us down to our most essential selves—to our flint hearts and Neanderthal DNA—as if we've been gnawed to bone and studs by locusts. Yet her essence seems to be forgiveness. These poems are at once New World and Biblical, quintessentially American, yet rooted in ancient myth laced with a quiet but fierce feminist thread unafraid to call out men's bad behavior, particularly those she shares blood with. The result is a wonderful poetic epic, both sensual and spiritual.

~**Lauren Scharhag, 2024 Rhysling Award winner and author of** *Ain't These Sorrows Sweet* **(Roadside Press)**

Accomplished poet Shelly Norris dedicates her collection *Dry Lake* "to the man who played my father in this life . . .". From that moment, readers realize that what we expect from relationships, resolutions, and reality is subject to upheaval. Norris sets most of her scenarios and speculations in the contemporary West. Thus, the poems lead us on a journey to real places such as highways, geographic landmarks, and features visible on maps. But some journeys can only be taken via memory, dreams, and emotion. Norris's storytelling voice, her sequencing of the concrete and the evocative, leads us to dwell on our personal narratives. Through her lyricism, we experience how the framework of language shapes ideas as clearly as landscape does.

~**Julianne Couch, author of** *Searching for Here* **(Horse Creek Studio)**

With ...*whose monochrome pasts are these? / ... / ...showcase of figurines no one's allowed to touch*, from *I Inherit Vitrine*, this collection of poems often reaches into the past to offer lessons on life that weave history into the author's present and leave the reader wanting more. There is much to discover in this collection. In *Grief Jumble*, Norris tells us, *I struggle to say what I mean, mean what I say, / so scrawl toward discovery through tangled loops / of slow deliberate script.* The poet invites us to follow those tangles to learn what shaped her, as she discovers in telling her stories, from the struggles between grief and acceptance or resentment and understanding, to the appreciation she expresses for lessons learned from others, as she eventually does from her father, telling us I *find comfort that the stolen pieces of his soul / he left behind make me laugh as he laughed / at misfortunes, so that when I reminisce / I feel more joy than sorrow.* The reader may learn as well, as *Abate, Worry!* tells us, *Unclench your knotted fists; / accept this gift of letting go.*

~**Ken Gierke, author of** *Glass Awash*, *Heron Spirit*, **and** *Random Riffs* **(Spartan Press)**

For Johnny Robert Norris
the man who played my father in this life,
for the helplessness and befuddlement
he experienced when I began to pay attention.

Contents of *Dry Lake*

Prelude to Exile

DRY LAKE

I wanted to say I don't belong
on this alkali flat water deserted.
Did any of us? Wanted to confide
I'm seldom at home, rarely at rest

in this vast ocean of body,
aimless, tidal, moon-towed,
at times a lethal force, mercenary
of shifting tectonic plates.

Wherever we are,
we wake to the same sad weather
we created yesterday.
Recycle the same clumsy blunders.

Thought if we relocated
rusted artifacts of wreckage,
restructured landscapes,
flooded over the sun -

bleached bones of rotted failures,
we could attract waterfowl
to teach us a way of being useful
and whole. Worthy of our space.

But we could not breathe
in that salt storm, averted our eyes
from what demanded more care
than we could afford,

closed our palms against
insufficient wet and abundant
cold offering snowflakes
dry as soda ash.

Embraced only our own bodies
to hoard what little heat
flint hearts could generate.
We stood so long

on that playa
waiting.
Petrified to white lime pillars,
only like life could grow from us.

But we were lovely out there,
luminescent by moon's light,
red veins pulsing litmus blue
beneath eerily green shells

so that we appeared
plausible.
Like we would not corrode
whatever suffered

our touch. Like we could
bear more loss.
Could still carry
the illusion forward.

Marlboro Country

A TETHER SNAPPED

In Memory of Robert Eugene Norris 1/30/1912 to 9/27/1986

I want to remember why
I was out early that day

before traffic, before farmers gathered
in the corner booth at Skyline for coffee gossip.

I want to remember the day—
was it Thursday or Friday—driving west

on Coulter Avenue, sunrise cresting the Big Horns
burning through soft frosted September air

glaring in my rearview mirror. Maybe
I'd gone out early to clean or shop and stock

for my shift later. I remember the voice:
Go see him now. Today's your last chance.

For the first time in my twenty-seven years
I was alone with him in that sterile room

just the two of us floating in white morning.
After four dramatic days, the novelty of his dying

worn thin, the others had disbanded to sleep
in their own skins. He lay alone, alert, and saw me

lurk in the doorframe, so there was nothing to do
but enter and sit beside his pain.

In the awkward silence, I took his heavy square
hand that sometimes slid places it shouldn't

and gave him words to leave by: *I love you.*
His grizzled brows arched. *You love me?*

I was surprised
at his genuine surprise.

What could I say but yes?
What could he say but why?

I'm not sure I loved him. Maybe. Once.
I'm sure I was supposed to.

Sure it was time to let go.
As the morphine tugged him under,

I laid his hand on the sheet. In the doorway
I crossed paths with my cousin twin also come

to say his good-bye. He'd heard the voice, too.
I never asked him what he might have to forgive.

WHENCEFORTH

I am from Johnny, Elvis debonair
dragging Main in his '56 Chevy Bel Aire.
James Dean grin, Marlboro man,
beloved of all the women.
I am from Peggy Ann, starlet stunning,
hourglass svelte, her 19-inch waist
cinched tight beneath that wide white belt.
Enchantress of needles and yarn,
she tried to stitch a world worthy of her
dreams. I am from these high school
sweethearts who didn't have to marry,
who, like a Hollywood couple
in a made-for-TV movie of the week,
destroyed each other from the inside out.
I am from Bob and Helen, who stuck it out
'til death from Round Up Hodgkin's Lymphoma.
I am from Gus and Oma Dee,
Okies drawn to Wyoming by oil,
parted too young by colon cancer.
I am from landed farmers, gentlemen
ranchers who were no gentlemen.
From oil field roughnecks, iron men
who manned the first wooden rigs.
I am from Andrew Jackson Shipman
born on Shawnee ground, from Dillie
Louise Self born to Arkansas sharecroppers.
I am from Brazoria Stevenson,
aunt of Sam Houston who failed the men
at the Alamo, first president of the Republic
of Texas ousted as governor for refusing
to side with the Confederacy.
I am from Eli T. Brison, a guard who died

and lies beside his prisoners at Andersonville.
I am from Civil War refugees
and dust bowl migrants and Depression
survivors who started over from scrap.
I am from Tennessee, Georgia, and Alabama
Rebs with no dog in the fight.
I am from Kansans allied to no side.
From Plymouth Puritans, Nauvoo Mormons,
hard-shelled southern Baptists,
and at least one Quaker. I am from
philanderers and scofflaws and bootleggers.
I am from lawmen who arrested their own kin.
I am from fornicators, adulterers,
and illegitimate lines. I am from
the southeastern coast of the New World,
from Virginia Territory,
from the salt mines, from Catherine
Rising Fawn Moytoy of Deer clan,
from Ghe no Heli Bushyhead of Paint Clan.
I am from the Trail of Tears.
I am from the Atlantic Ocean between worlds.
From all the isles west of the Old World.
From the Norse and the Danes
who invaded all the isles south of Scandinavia.
From Teutonic mercenaries
who fought them off.
Anthropologists say I am
out of Africa.
My DNA says I am from
Neanderthals.

LOCUSTS

Easy to imagine
it was imagination—
a child's concoction
of skeletons and closeted goblins—
as are so many memories.

Besides, such legends
must be documented
to count as legitimate
like that historically bitter
freeze of 1897 when entire

Angus herds solidified
in their tracks waiting out winter
like alabaster statuary
for spring's swollen rivers to freight
their bloated carcasses to no market.

Easier, I suppose, to speak casually
of history's and other people's tragedies
and perhaps it was—like the addictions,
arrests, adoptions, infidelities,
and infant deaths—reduced to statistics,

legal documents filed away
in bottom drawers, one more calamity
too difficult to admit into daylight.
Still, a neural loop in my brain
projects a flickering 8mm scene

where I witness a blackened sky
swarm down upon us, scarcely
hear above the maddened drone
everyone scramble indoors, my mind
mesmerized by that buzzing cloud.

How all around our shelter
the blackness shattered into bullets
pelting plate glass, rattling asbestos
shingles, assaulting our only safety
from the cherry orchard's gruesome fate.

The cloud abated
suddenly as it appeared. Then, how silent
hung the hostage sun and tattered boughs.
How tightly clung the bleeding cherry pits
stripped of their ruby flesh.

How the adults emerged defeated,
pooling eyes downcast, worried
wordless pats, and side eye glances
transmitting their harvest plans
for preserves and wine had been

gutted by that multitude of mandibles.
How we felt as though it were our skins
split, our flesh consumed, our stones
laid bare. How, like a brutal rape,
no one ever spoke of it.

MARLBORO MAN

You allow clandestine access, leave
the barn door ajar a scoche, just enough
to incite our curious minds to explore
the dark store of man-smelling tack.

From the cold hollow of your absence
we conjure a language
to guess at the secret
names of steel and leather parts:

bridle, halter, reign,
saddle, stirrup, bit, cinch.
Deep in our bones and sinew we know
full well the verb of each object.

Galloping out of the sunset
high astride your steed
you look handsome, vague,
down upon and through us.

We could mount and tame
wild mares in heat
yet never amount
to your legend:

Scofflaw riding herd into the saloon,
wind roper, star of the highway mural
who creates the sixteen-hand-high
ten-gallon hole in the Universe.

Serviceable heifers, we could be
bought and sold. Interchangeable
with every other broad,
you taught us our price.

Still, with a flick of ash, the toss of a butt
crushed beneath the heel of your boot,
you set us snarling against
each other like barroom bitches

while in a cloud of smoke you vanish
leaving a trail of dust impossible to follow.
Leaving the wind smelling of Canadian Mist,
Corinthian leather, wild yellow rose

AN EMBARASSMENT OF WILD PRAIRIE ROSES

Gangly, disheveled thickets sprout
beneath her east windows, harden
and bloom cold springs, thrive arid summers,
shed premature falls, sleep long bitter winters

by their own leave seeking no permission.
Disobedient, they titter secrets upon
hot breezes. Usurpers of boundaries,
they clamor leggy for sun, gulp scalding rays

like parched cattle traders. Canary yellow
and Pepto pink, they clash audaciously,
flaunt spare inadequate blossoms,
then strip tossing petals about

littering the immaculate lawn.
And for all these trespasses
display no shame! Worse, they love her—
love her not— as she'd planned to be loved

the way cultured well-mannered
American Beauties of her Camelot dreams
would love her, if only.
She sheared them, poisoned them,

burned them. To which they answered
burgeoning bolder, clashing louder,
refusing to tone it down. She turns her back
on their sass as they grow more brash,

to retire indoors where she paints
demure Victorian roses
in antiqued mauves and dulcet blues
on ceilings, walls, and window glass.

She arranges each stem and bud and bloom
in prim and proper poses on thorn-less canes
where they remain modest and never leave
without first politely excusing themselves.

NEO PURITAN

I slink into the shade under the eave
stewing in sweat and guilt
for wearing down before noon,
before I've planted the rest
of the cucumbers and thirty-two
squash starts bursting their peat pots.

When asked on which boat
his ancestors crossed the pond,
my Great Grandfather Merton John
Smith, a jack Reformed Latter Day Saint
who farmed Wyoming silt would state,
Our family met the boats.

His beliefs wavered between his parents'
faith shifting westward in handcarts
after Joseph Smith's assassination
and his fourth daughter's, my grandmother
Helen, who drifted Presbyterian.
She kept her garden immaculate.

Great Grandmother Norris
skewed Seventh Day Adventist,
but my grandfather Robert Eugene,
her secretly adopted son,
subscribed only to the Powell
Tribune and Sunday Billings Gazette.

From the other line,
Great Grandma Bonnie Jean
(née Eugenia) who changed
husbands, jobs, addresses, and
names when it suited her, embraced
her Texas Bible Baptist Jesus.

They all bequeathed
this common belief: Only hard work
renders one worthy of heaven.

LOVE APPLES: A ZUIHITSU

13

Across the yard, stray pear and cherry tomato vines
volunteer here and there, vestiges of haphazard
gardening forays. I say *vines*. He argues tomatoes
grow on a bush, as green beans do. Again, I say, *vines,
as green beans do.*

17

Cousin to deadly nightshades, our ancestors
on the isles *admired the tomato for its beauty
but believed it poisonous,* naming the fruit Wolf Peach.
In the US, the tomato *was not regarded as a kitchen
vegetable until the times preceding The Civil War.*

1

In the scrutiny of late summer stained-glass morning,
I clear spare kitchen counters, reclaim coveted work
surface from an entropy devoted to burying me in an
avalanche of clutter. In cardboard cartons next to a cool
air vent, dozens of tomatoes turn toward perfection.

2

My grandmother's kitchen belonged to her. She cleaned
up only after herself, no man spattering bacon grease
on her cast iron burners, upending milk glasses
in the stainless sink telegraphing through congealed rings
circular messages of hierarchy, order, division of labor.

14

Determinate tomatoes grow as a bush and ripen
all at one time; indeterminate tomatoes are produced
on a vine that grows continually producing tomatoes
from late summer until frost.
So, we are both right.

5

I lack acreage, tenacity, patience to grow enough fruit
to make preservation worth my sweat. Heartland gardens
and Amish greenhouses produce thousands of pounds
for sale at reasonable prices, heirloom varieties beyond
hybridized Beefsteak, Better Boys, Early Girls.

16

In high-altitude zone 4 Wyoming, frost comes
sometimes as early as late August. The women pluck
firm green fruits prematurely from withering vines,
carry them indoors in wire baskets to ripen upon
the society and obituary pages of the local Tribune
and Sunday Gazette spread on warm windowsills.

3

I quarter tomatoes bought by the bushel
from mid-Missouri Mennonites, crisp slits
through tight skins, firm red muscle glowing
bright as stop lights. Into oval enamel turkey roasters,
I mound dripping moons, skin, seed, and pulp.
Top with olive oil, roasted garlic, Kosher salt,
piles of homegrown rosemary, thyme, basil,
oregano, chives, parsley.

12

Lovers of light, seekers of heat, six to eight hours
of direct afternoon light is best. Plant only after frost
risk is past. In zone 4, this can be as late as June
and never as early as March.

4

From her west facing kitchen window, my grandmother
watched her garden flourish as she handwashed dishes.
Over fifty years of three meals a day: breakfast, lunch
of last evening's leftovers, and supper. *Dinner*
was a sacred meal, reserved for some Sundays,
holidays, and special occasions. She bore six children.
Every spring she planted six rows of tomatoes.

6

In high-altitude Wyoming, soil warms late.
Hardening tomato seedlings need protective structures,
wax-lined milk cartons with tops and bottoms excised,
tin coffee can collars rusted from years of use. Later,
wire cages to protect from gale force wind. Maybe hail.

7

Calculating the time they will take to roast down
to thick mash, I hear my German grandmother's
perturbed *tsk tsk.* I am never alone in my kitchen.
My method is not the way she would do it. *A-tisket,*
a tasket, I use no wire baskets, I left the kerchief
in her apron pocket where it dropped.

15

Depending on where one lives in Wyoming,
an expert says, the soil is either sand or clay.
Spend time amending. Condition with compost,
aged horse manure is best, peat, fertilizers.
Do this over and over.
All the good rinses away with the irrigation water.

8

In zone 4, it's usually October
before pounds of just ripened orbs are submerged
into rapidly boiling water then dunked into an ice bath.
Like a movie starlet coyly letting a pink satin robe
pour from her shoulders exposing, for maximum effect,
her perfect proportions, this once forbidden fruit
is stripped of its skin, quartered and seeded,
only the firm meat valued.

10

I watched the women boil out the goodness
and wash it down the drain, then press
the leached flesh through tiny sieve holes
with a wooden pestle, cranking the tool
around and around to separate the last fiber and seeds
yielding that soupy pulp my mother poured
over meat loaf, stuffed peppers, Swiss steak, spaghetti.

9

I only blanch and peel Romas to slip whole
into wide-mouthed quart jars. For sauce, blanching
is clearly more work than necessary. I treasure the fiber
and own a blender more powerful than any available
to my grandmother. I've no chickens to feed, so I grind
my roasted mash to buttery sauce thick as grits.

11

My roasting process tests true every run.
I still feel like a beginner, sense hammering
judgment from a chorus of ghosts seated on a ledge
like a clowder of cats. Spirits of people
who wore practical hats, worked the unpredictable
opera of outdoors, lived according to moods of manic
seasons. People who arranged parties more akin
to church services. People who couldn't vacation,
who could not bear ambiguity, could not sit quietly
amid the tight rope uncertainty of inertia.

I INHERIT VITRINE

Glossy grayscale specters float, worn corners
tacked atop black construction paper
pages; whose monochrome pasts are these?
Whose precious faces scrubbed shiny as
Vaseline glass? Whose older-than-their-years
brooding eyes project through a pixeled
spectrum of grays, the wear of hard times?
I can only guess. I never knew them.

See how, without those who remember, these
lives become some few trinkets posed and glazed,
unfocused, out of context, a distant
stranger's corner curio stationed
in the great hall where no one eats, showcase
of figurines no one's allowed to touch.

ELEGY ON PUGSLEY

Less than half a mile
down the road
my aunt's family
who didn't farm
kept a dog
the way town people do:
a considered decision
like someone who paid
attention in sex education,
not a homeless stray,
a puppy, not a vagrant,
a family member, not
night guard watch.
They trained him
to sit and beg and fetch
and let themselves love
him. While sleeping indoors
at the foot of their beds
he would not be shot
for packing up and chasing
sheep. My aunt taught him
to say *Mom.*
He died of old age.
A trick I did not know
a dog could do.

ONLY THIS SUN

Nowhere but this Paleozoic basin
does blistering August sun
elicit the electric hum
of summer days, sage-pungent,
milkweed-sweet absorbed within
spongy marrow pores of my bones,
bundled between the myofibers
layering muscle built pedaling
my bike over miles of tarry soft
unlined asphalt, drought-
powdered silt, and gravel roads.

Nowhere but this terraced valley
can I recall alfalfa scented air
abuzz with dragonfly wings,
melodious with Meadowlark trill,
the muffled timbre of faint echoes
as the ether swallowed our shrill
register of childhood wonder,
returning only partially
our deepening voices,
as dusk cooled its lush floor.

How far we ran, free and amok,
unreachable, answering our parents'
whereabouts inquiries with vagaries:
to the canal, to Dry Lake, to the river,
just down the back lane.
We secreted the private
detours through property
boundaries, down sideroads,
along ditch banks, to dead ends,
exploring every turn and thicket.

How innocent we were
to that privilege: farm kids,
country kids roaming wild
landscape at will, learning
the nature of each rock and weed,
the dens and lairs and hideouts
of animals that crossed our sight.

We knew nothing of cities, crowds,
poverty, urban blight, food deserts,
town people and outsiders who would
encroach to build mansions in bean fields.
We snacked at will from wild vines,
berry bushes, and fresh growth pilfered
from orchards and our mothers' gardens.

Each sunset we exited our
boundless Eden, disappeared
from each other's company stowed
behind unlocked doors concealing
each family's particular abuses.

DOWNSTREAM

Like gale force wind, frost, rust
and rugged self-reliance, like sunset,
antelope migration, cricket song
and suspicion of strangers,
like alkali, sage, stoic denial
and unpredictable Octobers,
Wyoming can depend on no rain.

Is this a good place to live? people ask.
By mid-July, corn, hollow-stemmed sunflowers,
Zinnias and Gerberas bend downward dog
while leathery bean leaves crisp and curl
their crenulated edges like rolling papers.
A country garden will wilt brown before
its weekly turn to drink from the reservoir.

The better question is
who thought this high desert a fruitful place
to farm? Before achieving statehood
some Washington wig proposed
partitioning this territory as the rivers run
into the four basins—roughly one-fourth
to Utah, to Colorado, to South Dakota, to Nebraska—

disrupting the quadrilateral geometry
of the West as we know it.
Saddled astride the Continental
Divide, before it can do much local work
three quarters of the water flowing within borders
drains toward greater endeavors:
The Bear tumbles to the Great Salt Lake Basin,

the Snake slithers and the Salt dissolves to the Columbia,
the Green and Little Snake join the Colorado
to erode a Grander Canyon, as the Yellowstone, Wind,
Bighorn, Shoshone, Tongue, Powder, Belle Fourche
Niobrara, North Platte, and Laramie Rivers rush like
refugees out to the Missouri and Mighty Mississippi
basins to flood and green America's heartland.

In service to the hot wind
and pesticide infected atmosphere,
the remainder translates to vapor
carried into the broad blue elsewhere
or seeps into alluvial and bedrock aquafers
where like shale oil, perhaps in the parched
future, it will be fracked out.

UNMOORED

Chill air churning with silt,
he let go in late September, finally,
my grandfather did,
as all around the green gold valley
field corn dried waiting to be chopped,
farmers thrashed grain, raked beans,
baled the last alfalfa cutting, and prayed
for early frost to spike sugar content of beets.

I wasn't there in the moment.
No one was there to witness.

From yards of crinkled navy rayon
speckled with white dots, discount fabric
purchased with no plan, I fashioned
a simple shift with an asymmetrical yoke
to wear to his funeral.
Classic, elegant, some of my best work.
Against that robe of star spattered midnight,
I wore the gray-veined agate heart
he fashioned for me in his lapidary phase.

If he were alive,
he would not notice or comment,
but my grandmother would
view it as homage.

With no saints for comfort,
no real god to blame or question or beg for mercy,
sewing all that long night eased an uncertainty.
What should any of us do now?

At the cemetery I wept.
I shrugged off sympathy's arms.
As autumn spiraled toward winter,
at last it seemed fine to speak the sacrilege:

I'm not happy here.
Fine to finally ask, *What comes next?*

Shadow Rider

SINS OF THE FATHERS VISIT: IN MEMORIAL

August 8, 2023

Perhaps it was not grimy greed,
that calculated grasp at absolute power.
Perhaps not heroics nor desire
to reign nor transcend to full god.
No doubt, he wanted only more
daylight for his children, longer cycles
of illuminated hours for art, for pleasure,
to invent shoes, to build an empire.

Dwelling annoyed in the absence
of color, in the dark wake left
as Sun trundled along
in haste—a daily rapid fire
short circuit full circle past
that place---unable to see
the supper bread before his face,
Maui schemed to control day.

Bypassing diplomacy or filing formal
grievance or observing traditions
of mutual negotiation, legend tells
how Maui and his brothers stole
into the ancient crater of Sun's
bed, ambushed the sleeping star,
bound him in enchanted flax ropes,
and beat him about jowl and brow
with a magic ancestral jawbone
until exhausted from the tussle,
with resounding defeat, Sun
agreed to stroll each day

at a more leisurely pace
across their basalt raft.

But this, we know, is not the end
of this story. An abused Sky Spirit
has a limit to the disgrace He
will endure. Centuries Sun brooded
pacing his track, replaying the humiliation,
the travesty of disrespect, dangling along
biding terms of the coerced treaty.
Shedding his begrudged gift, he enlisted
mortal meddling to design rife conditions
to wreak vengeful devastation.

Drawn as moths to that dreamy
temperate paradise, Conquerors waded
ashore, grasped the land
as irreverent thieves, built the wheels,
set ticking the machinery of annihilation.

And suddenly, after patient eons,
within mere decades, the stage set to perfection:
symbiosis between green sugar cane
and dense pineapple foliage photosynthesizing
Sun's generous rays to lush ground cover
disappeared giving way to wild grasses
that brittled instantly at His touch.

Defiant, He flared, sucked the last drops
of moisture from the air, burned
away the rain for days upon days.
He hung out heating the atmosphere
brewing up a hurricane
to topple the teetering electric wire.

One spark is all He needed
to set his anger loose on Maui's
innocent children.

A devastation now more than legend.
One, we hope, is not Maui's final defeat.

IPHIGENIA'S LAMENT

Born adrift a grass ocean bathed in incessant wind
to a father who could not stomach killing a hind,
and for as long as I have known him been at war,
he taught me I am a woman not worth fighting for.

The young men found me motherly, the old men
daughterly. My own father, objectionable with feet
too long and mind too broad. Exiled to a faraway land,
I asked four holy men the purpose of my suffering.

The Priest proposed pain as incentive to seek
his generous God. The Imam declared my agony
birth's well-deserved punishment, a blessed
gift from his harsh and violent Allah. In kind,

the Monk assured no need to suffer if only
I learn to open my hands. Sorrow is, he claimed, a choice.
The Hindu spoke from an ancient place in a lyrical voice:
Suffering, child, is merely your path to wisdom.

Still, I keen this tale in the key of betrayal. The bargain
he drove when I was no longer the virginal glory of his
home, not but useless currency. About what happened
next, those witnesses who looked askance yet refuse to say.

STUDY OF SHELL CANYON

The ice stays late, still
girds the creek's jagged edges.
From muskeg glens, wild
lupine and columbine begin
to bloom, random lacy petals
stenciled to a cerulean sky,
a blue so saturated
its light stings my eyes.
A crowd of tall stems tower
above greening buffalo grass,
wobble as impermanent
caricatures in a hot breeze.
They drink deeply
the immortal sunshine
their dominion here so brief.
Fanning frilly petals in pinks
and lavenders, their delicate
hues echo those of multi-layered
strata the creek's exposed over eons:
gray-blue limestone, gray-green
siltstone, gray-pink granite; soft,
earthy rusted and algae hued shale;
sky white, river blue and variegated
red spectrum dolomite.
Force fed rapidly melting snowpack,
the raging icy creek slices
down,
down,
down.

SUNSTROKE

That last leaden day sank into the dungeon
with tremendous keening. Like a question
drawn and quartered. Not the same sound
as the heart confessing its ancient wounds
which came later and lasted eons.

On cue, the moon crowned, lighting a path
up the staircase laden with amethyst
and aquamarine. Eternally brilliant!
She ascended to her silver zenith
whence moonbeam seeped beneath the floor

of the ocean transforming it to a magnificent mirror.
And to everywhere the enemies scattered:
all the restless Vices who had centuries gone
stolen the world's spirits and souls, who only meant
to borrow but then carelessly mislaid the bended knees

clasped hands, and lips pursed in fevered prayer.
They did this in gold daylight whereby they masqueraded
as married prostitutes and holy pimps crusted in sequins.
Before this, countless days frittered in sameness
by those idle spirits so unlike (we always imagined)

our crippled selves. Also, clearly, I was never immune
like you. Although, like you I could not recognize my fault.
Fragmented, ignorant, my only desire for stability
which is nothing but illusion.
Still, light would not return for many revolutions.

And even so, the world could never turn
back to as before. Many nights the enemy regrouped
hair bleached and spiked, throats encircled
in battle torques, their leader bent on reclaiming this territory.
But the ocean's secrets belong to the splendid moon

revealed only to those who study their reflections.
And what about those other projections
lost and forgotten
which never even depended
upon our memories for existence?

Yet, for that time they amounted to everything
we knew we were. Now, left standing
in this same weedy field with no evidence
of acceptance, we can never know each other's
true inclinations.

WAKING RAW

Somewhere between sleep's centrifuges
and daybreak's coagulation, the small fire
suffocated to the rhythm of the leaky faucet's
flat plinking waltz. Outside, afternoon footsteps
crackle parched leaves, carry rootless voices

that peel past the open window's torn screen
with the Velcro zip of bare flesh separating
from a pea green waffled Naugahyde sofa bed
forced upon us by an old lover. Hinges squeal
as the door opens and two blank figures exit

shuffling, dragging a hollow human pelt
between them. The first thought curdles
toward the cracked plaster ceiling like toxic smoke.
The next thought scabs over, dry and black.
Mercifully, no light, no air enters.

It has been this way every morning since
the sun, spinning down out of the sky,
collapsed into the basement
searing our eyelids, singeing our lashes,
roasting us out of our old skins.

If we could speak, what would we say?
Nothing fits anymore? The wires pinch?
This is all for our own good?
None of it is true
all of the time.

To breathe in this state
is to risk combustion.
Neither of us is prepared to surrender.
If either of us leaves this room today
I'm going out alone.

THE UNCONVENTIONAL GRAMMAR OF DREAMS

She spends
a priceless collection of nights
in a cluttered secondhand shop
culling through shelves of trinkets and knick-
knacks, not sure what she seeks, and leaves
with nothing but a sense
that the location of lost articles
is indefinite. Mysterious
segues move the action forward
as one bizarre prepositional scene dissolves
into the next: in a bathroom, next to a sink,
on the phone, beside a river (running along a riverbank).
Seemingly, these directions are conjunctive keys
connecting point there to point here
linking dependent fragments.
This Dreamer and the woman
chasing her demand an equal share
of whatever is to be discovered, even
though, perhaps, they are the same woman.
I like your hair! shouts the woman chasing.
The running Dreamer agrees with the compliment,
though not the demand. A plurality, singularly
they have always lived in subject-pronoun
antecedent disagreement.
Finally, in a deserted village, where one church bell
sways silent and feather-light amid a noiseless wind,
only a congress of mottled horned owls
perched atop the terra cotta roofs of adobe houses
signifies an absurd sort of unity.

SHADOW RIDER

The first sighting he appeared at dusk.
Just stood there, statuesque
on the shoulder of my childhood
lane upwind of my father's lover's house.

Outfitted in black boots, black Levi's,
and a black V-neck T-shirt, his long wavy hair
and black canvas duster flared out like terrible
wings. He was a vision of virgin androgyny.

Lame in the left leg, his right hand crippled,
tenderly he gestured toward November's
fallow fields where the image of a stag's head
loomed behind him like a halo, and desire

became the sinew binding my bones.
But then he began to shift. An evasive
self-publishing peer from graduate school,
he forced his way into the old house on Bent Street

where the affair began, drank
my father's whiskey decanter dry
and bounced tennis balls off the walls
waking my mother from her ignorant coma.

Out on the street corner, beneath the halogen
lamp waning in the dawn, he seized
from alcohol poisoning. After reviving him,
I knew he would have to die.

Some nights he arrives as an anonymous General
rattling about in antique armor, girded in black mail.
Perhaps Agamemnon with his captive mistress Cassandra
in tow, searching out his escaped firstborn daughter

Iphigenia to sacrifice again for his fleet's smooth sailing.
Some nights he wears a black leather vest and Stetson.
He comes as Will Smith, a synthesis of *Enemy of the State*
And *The Wild, Wild West*, deliberately stalking

down a deserted street, spurs chinking,
silver pearl-handled Colts drawn,
sweetly singing my name to coax me out.
He is trying to find me.

Last night he was the U.S.
Marshall Wyatt Earp: Kurt Russell in *Tombstone*
and the line between law and scofflaw blurred,
the distance between him and me closed.

He's mounted now, fully outfitted in his black
ten-gallon triple-X Stetson, black Wranglers, black
snakeskin Tony Llamas, black Outback duster,
leather holster, pearl-handled forty-fives.

Gathering momentum and audacity,
he's dogging me, tracking me like prey,
running me down like bounty, trying
to wave me over like an express rider

delivering a letter
that I forgot
years ago
I mailed to myself.

MEMO

There is no room for an other
in this tangled bed. Last night I sat around
the table, at least five of me, drunk
and incoherent, discussing the complex
in platitudes, formulating simplistic solutions
to the Sphinx's ancient riddle.

Many such meetings have convened—on the set,
behind the scenes, in secret internal monologues
playing through static air. Recently,
a lithe young woman from an unknown country
was transformed to smoke and ash inside
the wicker giant; thus, sparing her short fat twin.

Some of us now agree: We may be
nearing some resolution, which is just a word
one letter removed from sudden and radical
renunciation or the progressive rotation of heavenly
bodies. Either or both are imminent
and acceptable. At any rate, we won't know.

Until the old woman sitting lotus on the hill
pulling thin gold chains from the world's
largest knot manages to unravel that last
double hitch, finally undoing the labyrinth.
Not for all time.
At least for once and again.

SOME MORNINGS

Some mornings barrel in head on
careening straight out of the mineshaft
hauling up the night shift and unordered cargo.
Inside the echo of clattering cars
still loaded with yesterday's steaming slag
a semi-consciousness anticipates

orchestration—some sort of birdsong
to herald the onrush, expects to crest
into firelight atop the refrain of some cosmic love
song, some sudden insight— and wonders
Where are the flutes?
Where are the violins?

Belying still dusky surfacing seconds,
a memory—of a candle flame of an ancient age,
of a piccolo's shy lilt— casts a merry shadow
along stuccoed walls, dances about the notion
that we could remain forever here
in this half dream slide stepping sideways.

Everyone's intentions are good.
Perhaps settling wouldn't be so bad.
But then a meadowlark's trill reminds
what has taken lifetimes to learn:
The sun is not called, but summons.
It is we who tunnel underground

seeking fortunes and burrow away
from the gods. Each day's new business
is about nothing less than recovering.

PUCE

This morning smells of wet iron.
The air tastes of chew-worn liver and blood.

All night we backtracked into the dark
purple-brown and red-brown shadows
down into the thick wood, cautiously stepping
over the rotting headless auburn carcasses
of four moose: a cow, yearling twins, a calf.

We searched the decaying leaf-strewn
forest floor for the rack of the bull.
No sign. Damn him!
He escapes every time. Still,
now something new can begin.

Emerging from the old
blood-heavy shadows, the dense dark
saturated with all color and sound,
we arrive at a pink dawn-lit ridge
overlooking that gully of death.

We know the cabin here
is ours. But someone's left
the sofa sleeper rummaged, packages
of ground meat souring in the fridge,
a bin of putrefying cucumbers and cabbage.

As we begin to clean away the rot,
a stranger comes to warn us.
Higher up this mountain, deeper
into the forest lives a Red Prince
who believes this house is still his.

She says we can expect more trouble.

TRICKSTER

after Paisley Rekdahl

You will die.
You will die hide and skiff, daguerreotype and pistols.
You will die sepia denim and telegraphing
all the assorted trauma communiques: clenched fists
and kicking stones, averted eyes and crossed arms,
just like most men hold themselves
close and closed and closeted saving their secret
best parts for some white-haltered centerfold
fantasy to sashay across the air vent
of the entitlement they hide beneath. You will die
the way seasons die, malingering
and milking time for more of it, your toe grip on earth
uprooting as you rip away. You will die
as thousands of cumuliform clouds
that touched ground then turned on themselves
to spin out have died, wispy, milky trails dissipating
to topaz; the way a housefire sends tapestry
and wood skyward, crackling like static neural relays.
You will die dark and meteoric and to applause.
You will die cowardly as you imagine a girl, the way
no girl would allow herself, the way the humble dare not
consider, for to be the center of such attention
is to invite scrutiny. Hermaphrodite
of death, Kahli of death, Shiva of death; this is how
you will die, roots and mildew and mud.
You will die with no dog and as an orphan. You will die
as your friends starve, beside the fat craters
of the shelled moon. You will die in this dream and the next
and the next. You will die as all of them one by one
and all at once. You will die

as me—know this, I have already died a hundred deaths—
and the impossibility of continuing infantile and splintered
should ferry the lot of us to some safe harbor.
You will die
the way the charred forest dies,
dormant beneath its carpet of ash,
reconsidering spirit, reconsidering sprout,
reconsidering intimacy
to altruism and sworn servitude.
You will die each time you chase me down
screaming my name as if to ensure your legacy:
Yes; you were, you were, I will always remember,
even as you disintegrate into random flashing pixels
spinning apart in a centrifuge of confusion.

VECTORS

The Gash, Big Horn Mountains, Wyoming

A random fleck, you stand in ruptured day-
dream, a terminal point atop a fault
on a foothill where arid stressed earth cracked
herself open. Jacquard hues, a spectrum
of mauves and taupes, stack as delicate striations
on vertical slants. The divorced crevice walls
are not estranged. Do not abandon each other.
Steep sides work together to keep a continent
from tumbling into the fissure, each strike-slip
bolsters, one holds north in place, the other
south at bay, each scarred face a torn photograph
of eons, a history to be read by those
who know this language etched by time.
Back lashed against perpetual gales

bristling your torso, you stand, lodgepole rigid,
long gaze trained westward carrying hundreds
of miles of magnitude. The velocity of a glance
carries split recognition. Like this mound of land,
you have no immunity against sorrows
that burrow labyrinths of tunnels, against yearning
that seeps into every chamber weakening foundation,
against the distance between your feet planted
at this crumbling ledge and memory pooled
behind those mountains. Schools of silver trout
leap momentarily into cerulean death
then arc to safety in the black-green lake depth,
the rainbows of their brief flights shimmering,
inklings on the wind.

Confessions of a Solar Daughter

CALENDULA

Honeyed grace and copper tremor,
orange filament and gold plate,
mahogany shoulders, brass button,
hybrid elusive red frill longing to lust:
Call me Zoe, the least
beloved daughter of Midas.
Mark my evolution not for
his folly and infidelity
but for my introverted self
wandering lone but not lonely
among market crowds,
a wizened face of time
effusing scent of spirits
from deep sun-sated pockets,
protector of cabbages and carrots,
healer of fever, scald, open wounds,
disruptor of big round lies, acolyte
paying tribute at altars and shrines
once a fair substitute for coins,
my ability to thrive anywhere,
foster and reseed
a golden garland wreathing earth.
True, I am not
for everyone. Prevaricators & lovers
of fuchsia. Beware my double walker,
common ragweed; be not fooled
when she calls herself Ambrosia
Artemisiifolia. Ah, and tries to pass
as harmless; she'll infest your visions,
strangle you in your sleep, light
your skin afire. Reconsider our liaison:
If you wish to carry me for hope

and unity and October remembrance
of your dead, you must also
accept the way I gather overnight
grief into my ruffled skirts, the way
I sparkle with mourning by morning,
and flush with sunshine return
taller, fuller, spare of blossoms
to take your full measure
all passion and jealousy,
joy and despair.

ASTIGMATISM

Look; it's not like I don't try to see
The Universe in the wonky elliptical
curvature of this avocado pit.

Or don't try to recognize fragments of myself
in a splendid multi-gemmed mosaic fanning
and folding in the wide end of a kaleidoscope—

triangular shards of emerald envy, a rhombus
of ruby ego, cubes of citrine cowardice, squares
of rose quartz innocence, decagons of aquamarine

dreams, a perfect circle of amethyst armor,
and heptagonal cubic zirconia possibility—
shattered facets of my origins beautified

in their distortions. I can nearly make out among
blurred shadows, there in a large animal's decaying
carcass—in the flesh shrinking from its bones,

in the hide peeling away abandoning the raw muscle
it sheltered, in all of the parts struggling to salvage
themselves from each other's fate—my own

transformations, not romantic, not desired.
It's not as if I don't try to forgive my parents'
infidelities as I meander in the leaf-fractured

light swimming disparate yet unified into the forest's
depths like epipelagic fish foraging upon the air---
a school of shimmering inklings

bobbing between bottom and shore.
I try to see some kind of divinity here.
But honestly; peering into cold gray deep

moments shuttered in time trying to imagine
how they might have been once—
rain pure and bursting green, resilient,

happy with hope and delirious with expectation
like this finally spring—it's like peering through
the wrong end of binoculars with my good eye closed.

VENEER

I can, with considered reflection, forgive
the Depression-era wardrobe doors
for their buckled oak facades overlaying
some unidentified inferior wood, peeling
up the center as if pried loose by desert air

as I can forgive a German grandmother
slapping that last dried cheddar cube
out of my hand and swallowing it *for god's
sake* before I fed it to the trash because
give it here— we don't waste food!

Of necessity the wardrobe's overlay parallels
so many stories of the simple country folk
gone to town or church or court or graveyard
worn and sturdy and serviceable under thin
pretentious suits, dressed as something they weren't.

I couldn't forgive the plastic wagon wheel molding
and faux black walnut bonded by industrial glue
to the honesty of a raw cedar hope chest
and the white room dressed in yards and yards
of pink gingham and eyelet Little Bo Peep ruffles.

More recently, I can't forgive laminates posing
as fine hardwoods. Spongy and easily gouged
and impossible to polish like the polite smiles
and ma'ams of leering Royal Air Force recruits
behind sheer veils of social decorum,

with which Americans rarely bother, phony
manners that erode thinner with each warm pint
until ale brash the unrefined boor shows through.
I can't forgive fake wood paneling darkening and dat-
ing rooms, concealing imperfections and needs

of load bearing walls, and molded resin frames
protecting images of ersatz families. I can't forgive
plastic parading as cut glass, olefin pretending its
wool, Naugahyde passing itself off as leather,
cubic zirconia claiming the same properties

as diamonds or genuine crystal, the invulnerable
the long-wear suffering, the always-new
the too shiny, too perfectly colored flawless
like Cher's eyelids and lips,
like Tom Cruise's new smile.

FAILING FENCE

Well I recall the hands
that built the fences:
young bucks from town,
wrestlers paid to work out,
their bicep-powered hands
gouging post holes into
sunbaked dry earth, manual
machines driving down
wood posts, stretching a net
of wire for miles, their dry,
cracked, calloused hands
ratcheting the tension
drum tight so that wire sang
a low D sharp against
icy north winds.

So much labor spent to box in
desolate prairie, the exact same
rusted browns inside as out.
No green anywhere. Such folly
to section acres in uniform geometry,
an offense to the eternal feminine.

No engineered division can stand up
to constant assault—elk and deer
herds vaulting, wind piling snow
like dunes on a shore. Subject to laws
of gravity, taut wire pressures posts
to lean, to ease sharp angles
to comfortable slack. Buffalo grass
climbs a barbed trellis claiming
any empty space and the north
mossed cedar posts soften toward decay.

MOVING ROCKS

A sunny spring Saturday
with chores out of the way,
I pulled my red Radio Flyer
out to the barn drive ditch
and loaded it with dark gray
rocks, sedimentary conglomerates
composed of minerals cemented
by silica, calcite, iron oxide,
large stones rounded smooth
during transport to the valley
that was once sea floor.

One by one, I smashed
rock against rock, cracking
them open to discover shiny
white quartzite, gleaming mica,
pinkish feldspar, glinting
pyrite flecks. Fool's gold:
I thought I'd struck it rich.

What on earth—are you doing!?
my father asked more perplexed
by this activity than most
I devised. I didn't know.
Couldn't tell him why
I needed to move them, found
such glee in dividing these
ancient treasures, exposing
their secret inner lives.

A couple of decades later
on a warm summer day
in Anthropology 101, I learn
that humans and chimps
and labradors instinctively
move rocks from place to place.
Some dogs even build cairns.
I ask the professor why.
Can't really say, he says.

TOO BIG FOR MY BRITCHES

Certainly, they meant the idiom
about the sass spit
from my smart Alec puss—
Miss no-manners, Miss no-filter,
Miss speaks-her-mind,

Miss inappropriate-
question-asker, Miss talks-
too-much, Miss just-be-quiet—
but there was
that other rather obvious

backhanded backside reference:
Your little sister
doesn't split
the zippers
in her jeans!

My father fussed over his slender
fingertips fidgeting over my jeans
to realign the teeth chain,
to reconnect the retainer box
creating the bottom stop.

Serviceable for some hours
the work never held, just
as taping my mouth shut
or slapping me silent
would never hold.

SASSAFRAS FLASH

I trace ancestors to Essex, Wessex, Sussex,
Middlesex—who wants to talk that much sex
or Saxon invasion—godless Germanic heathen
bands raiding up and down the languid North
Sea Coast, pillaging serfs, raping as pay?
Who wants to factor what percentage

of renegade blood and magenta matter survives
in my fractal helix? The cosmology of their history
that isn't murky is unwieldy, certainly not taught
in public education on Fridays to goofy jokers
destined to mature into potbellied good ol' boys
from guzzling refrigerated kegs and before that

whose naked post-graduation antics
got the Pioneer Club downtown dubbed
"The Zoo." Bridging grade school and junior
high, those boys made it their mission
to entrance and deflower every uncloistered
town girl, those with and especially those

without pedigree. All on the same baseball team—
a hard scrabble gang with big-dog personalities—
they spent that hot season colluding how to score
by organizing pubescent orgies at the eastside
ballpark behind the batting cage or how to brush
against anything girl on the mowed grass mattress

between the nine-foot chain link fence
and the dugout. The whole team lapsed
into a slump—Babe Ruthers—some of them
scrapping star-bright futures for a potential lay.
The ringleader twins, descended from Scottish
Clan MacGilleMhoire, servants of Mary, the most abject.

A week after school let out, on report card day
I rode my Pinto pony Sugarfoot into town
to gather the document bearing my D- in science.
The twin whose name means church begged to ride my horse.
Crass as he was, I wanted him to like me, so I let him.
After all, what boy doesn't long to be a maverick.

Beneath his foreign scent, muscular weight,
and untutored hand, she reared. Dumped him on the asphalt
street like a mildewed dishrag. Later, my dad would tell me,
most men really need a saddle. I walked to where he lay
writhing upon his back, took the reins, mounted up
bareback, and trotted home with my virginity.

HEIMWEIH

It's cliché: I didn't pine for home
until my parents declared bankruptcy
and irreconcilable differences,
until the auctioneer parceled out the farm
implements for the price of seed and the land
returned to the bank that always owned it.

Until my mother took my brother and moved
to Oklahoma to become a library scientist.
Until my father began squirming in and out
of his stable of girlfriends. Until a banker
bought the place, razed the stucco house,
and built a new one, front door facing east.

Until, done roaming the planet,
I returned from Alaska with no landing
strip. Until my father, who'd finally settled
into my grandparents' house with his new
wife told me, *I don't know where
you'll go; you can't stay here.*

Friends who visited me over relocations
noted, *Everywhere you go, you make it
home.* I had a system: acquire furniture, lay
down rugs, nail up photos, the only way I knew
to ground inside someone else's walls
in foreign towns easy to leave in the rear view.

GRIEF JUMBLE

I am so weary, a philosophy professor
opined, *of seeing students spell 'existence'*
with an 'a'.

At the beginning of the root
or the beginning of the suffix? I inquire
to lighten the pall and display
my mastery of irony and linguistics.

He did smirk. He's long dead,
this academic who introduced me
to the European Magical Realism
of Gunter Grass, Thomas Mann's
reluctant Modernism, Nietzsche's
Nihilism, Kierkegaard's Existentialism
and Descartes' formula
for determining am-ness, all
which fundamentally reordered
the trajectory of my exi-stance.

Don't apologize. Life is a journey of grievances:
a wasp moved into the birdhouse I fashioned
for a swallow or a finch; my chief complaint
about canines is they don't live long enough;
then, neither do too many children, and if they do,
the veils between them and war, them and disease,
them and prison are sheer. We see how locked
doors protect no one, particularly innocents.

We have every right. It's hardly fair to compare
dogs to children, wasps to swallows, the rampant
cell division of disease spinning tumors
as efficiently as wasps build a hive. One life
to another—I don't mean to imply the word value—

I struggle to say what I mean, mean what I say
(so scrawl toward discovery through tangled loops
of slow deliberate script). Any which way, it is
impossible to define natural causes, as demise is
the natural consequence of life.
Life the cause of death.

It's not just losses. The condition of grief is bloated
with hardships, suffering, pain, physical
afflictions, wrongs, injustices, calamities. Guilt
over grief is guilt over existence.

Grief is not a shrine we enter and exit at will,
not a place we camp, a bivouac
at the base, the way we speak
of abiding briefly, then surmounting
the insurmountable and moving on.

Grief is a mobius of sorrow
we dwell inside which dwells within us,
a swarming hive layering a malignant growth
metastasized at the heart that can't be excised.
An intricate delicate web with the deceptive
strength of Kevlar. There's no comparing
yours to mine. Stop.

No wonder we prefer to shun it,
ignore it, organize the cabinets,
change the sheets, subjugate it
to a season
of migrating emotions,
hummingbird highs
and grounded gaggles of geese
that don't hang around for long.

Anthropomorphize all manner
of trees as metaphors of mourning
weeping leaves, or drunk talk
over it at the wake, or learn
like my Athabaskan neighbors
in Fairbanks to Stomp Dance
it into the earth. There's more:

Under threat of breakdown, I spoke
at her memorial, my friend says,
because I had stuff to say. I can't
speak at ceremony, can't read,
can't sing without disintegrating.
Not that I don't have stuff to say.
I have stuff to say.

I CAN'T SING AT THE FUNERAL

To maintain a vibrato from lapsing into sobs is a discipline I will never master. I can't even read aloud most poems or Karaoke *Forever Young* without choking up. This is a knowing gleaned from decades of trying and failing. I'd planned to sing Christine McVie's *Songbird* at my oldest son's wedding. The moment Gevorg stroked his rosined bow across the strings of his vintage violin toning a lone-string rendition of a ballad by NIN as my son watched his bride float down the aisle, a clod of tension damming a river of sobs burst. I was so overwrought, my granddaughters standing next to me began sobbing as well.

I signaled to Jun, the pianist, I would not be singing the song we'd practiced a dozen times.

After D'Lynn's suicide that late September, at her service held in the funeral home, not the church, probably because she'd once set it on fire, and also because she took herself out with a .45 she picked up at a pawn shop, I tried to render my part of the duet we'd performed so many times year after year at summer camp where we met each other as unacceptably boisterous twelve-year-old girls. The first five ascending notes—*Lay your burden down*—gagged me. I couldn't recover. Couldn't do it without her 12-string accompaniment, without her harmony. But I kept trying. Should have taken my seat. Sucking back sobs center stage made my grief seem heaviest and embarrassed the congregation.

The music at funerals is usually pretty awful. The vocalist at my Aunt's memorial forgot to breathe and pitched lyrics in a different key than the electric piano player's accompaniment. It was painful.

That October after my grandfather passed, my grandmother walked me down the quiet gravel lane under those yellowing cottonwoods that are gone now and stated in her nonsensical way, "I want you to sing *In the Garden* at my funeral." This demand was an affirmation of my existence I could not refuse. So, I promised, even though I didn't really know the song or how I'd get through it when the time arrived.

I had nine years to prepare for a moment for which we can never really prepare. The soft- frosted October morning she passed just days after her 84th birthday, my grandmother reminded me in a waking vision of her and I cutting fuchsia petunias from her garden to grace the lunch table. I saw my five-year-old self standing next to her tall lean figure bent over the silky petunias she always planted on the end row where she could view them from the kitchen window. Her dress and apron fluttered in a hot breeze as she clipped hot pink and white trumpet blossoms and placed them in the basket I held. When I came around from that reverie, I knew she'd passed before anyone reached me with the news. That's how she held me to that promise.

At her funeral, my father's stepdaughter with the same name as mine stood at the side lectern and belted out *Amazing Grace* in a soulful alto acapella to rival my idol, Linda Rondstadt. She didn't crack once. But it wasn't her grandmother lying in the casket at the bottom of the steps. Three decades before, I'd stood on this very dais to sing *Evergreen* at my cousin's wedding. At sixteen, I was no Barbara Streisand, but if I remembered to breathe deeply into my diaphragm and closed my eyes, I could do the song justice, as long as I didn't look anyone in the face. That's how I learned to sing in church: Don't look. That's why I didn't make Pop Group in high school. "Why do you close your eyes when you sing?" one red headed boy mocked. To glance into the eyes of the people seated in the front pews would melt me to a useless gurgling puddle. So, I sat low behind the pulpit and crooned into a microphone.

"As if your voice descended from above," my mother later spoke, "that's when your father broke down."

Over a decade later, out on Willwood under waning cottonwoods singing *Angel* and *Amazing Grace* for my soul twin's mother, and also my Aunt who passed just before and whose memorial music disappointed, I gazed above everyone's scalp and sang to the quaking leaves of a lone Aspen, never registered familiar and unfamiliar faces before me or my divorced parents seated beneath my right elbow. I'd gathered the instrumental tracks, speakers, microphones, and practiced the dulcet Irish glides a hundred times. I'm not bragging; it was beautiful. People wept.

My father turned to my mother who once told me I couldn't carry a tune in a bucket: "Well" he seemed genuinely surprised, "I guess we haven't heard her sing for quite some time!"

" No," I told him later when he approached me with a hug to convey his pride in me, his oldest child, a pride that came far too late to register points in my self-esteem column.

"No, what?" His graying brows furrowed slightly.

"No, I will not sing at your funeral. You can't ask

65

that of me." He nodded, seeming to know what I meant.

I arranged the best for his service: the sonorous tenor acapella of a volunteer fireman who was a football hero and a choir star when we were in high school together; the Patsy Cline intonations of my cousin's wife who sang a song she wrote about Heart Mountain, along with *That Silver Haired Daddy of Mine*. They performed flawlessly.

The December day before my father passed, I sat next to his hospital bed all day holding his hand. Clear as Sunday church bells, I sang every hymn I know from the Pentecostal indoctrination forced into me by my mother: *Rock of Ages, Old Rugged Cross, I'll Fly Away, Swing Low, Sweet Chariot*, and of course, *Amazing Grace*. I sang some twice. The reverberation in the nearly empty chamber amplified my voice with pure resonance as his heart monitor beeped like a metronome.

Beyond the curtained cubicle on the fourth-floor critical care unit, I didn't care who heard. I know he did.

TOPOGRAPHY OF A SILENCE

Here we are again, a shallow
brooding inactive caldera.
Saddled with paniers
full of rocks and grudges
but no tools for survival, dangling
from frayed daydreams
of now unwanted fame.

Afraid to rappel,
we could die here: defective carabiners
unraveling ropes, my spatial deficit
for learning knots.
If searchers find us
they will not identify the bodies
too badly broken, carrying false ID.

We knew this would happen.
Knew it every day. Said this would happen.
Imagined the precipice in daylight.
Lived and relived the drop each night.
These lines are true, aero triangulated
for accuracy, checked against survey values
and cultural standards, keeping in mind

imprecision and rightness
are not the same and details relative
to anyone. How well one follows the discrete
signals determines degrees of social veracity.
How effortless one makes it appear
measures degrees of image verisimilitude.
Our baseline reference is the comfort

level of the cartographers in the room.
Ours feared all features within and beyond.
Between white boundaries of absolute
arable land and the black absolute navigable
waters, the vast frontier in shades of gray
was and always is unspoken.
It may be brackish marshland;

Those who venture beyond fail
to return. We do not like
the uncivilized appearance,
the primal, restless sound of it:
Bad things happen there.
Or did once.
Or could again.

Label that territory quicksand.
Speak of it no further.
We will likely reside
in a desert of scarcity
challenging this established terrain
or the overgrown rain forests of excess
never questioning.

I BEGIN TO WRITE

When people laughing one day
vanished the next.

When scaffolded excuses collapsed
into mountains of immovable debris.

When questions were accusations,
answers construed as confessions.

When words I needed
hid beneath fears I could not name.

When the forests around us burned,
when earth slipped from beneath my soles.

When the wolves and buffalo
and bears were so few.

When anyone who uttered the word
love left a wake of destruction.

When one day a teacher granted
permission to scribble my truth.

Because when I lifted pen from page
the storm smattered world outside

still sang and bloomed.

CONFESSIONS OF A SOLAR DAUGHTER

I stole those things:
The King's minted silver coins and the Debutante's
molded sugar basket, sweet collectable souvenirs of Camelot;
the fermenting liquid cherry-centered chocolate gifts;
the soft, still-warm pelts of slaughtered pets.
Oh, and this; the rhythm and tone of the demented
priest's song. I hid them here.

From where you are
you can't see 'hem
multiplying. As if I were indestructible. No one intercedes
anywhere for me. The trees, why even the trees masquerade
in ways I understand and loathe.

Brushing my henna hair in the rain, finally. I know your god
is not a woman. He does not flame. He is unfriendly
and indifferent. He is too small.
Concealing from me the sky and road: these buried
in ice. Divinity ignores me and smolders like the smoke
of cold fire inside its own eternal
absence.   So many years I wandered.

Before all of this, the destructive and informal jugglers
walked off the stage dragging their blunt and hollow toys.
I couldn't instruct them then, but I can now—
because of making up for the lost
dreams. They surface and press;
naked, I smile and juggle and they juggle in the solar eclipse
wearing my old costumes. They crown me
Queen of the Living.

ABATE, WORRY!

Feckless thief, you've nicked enough
time and sleep and metaphor.
Bloody perfectionist, thwarted
too many beginnings.
Spoiled imp, interrupted more
than your share of revery.

Remember those August days
dressed in cut-offs and halter tops
sailing bikes on a hot breeze?
No thought of the goat head
that would puncture the tire,
no concern for sun burning flesh

until the sting squirmed like fire ants
from the pores of our scorched skin.
Walking bikes home in cool dusk
rising from the irrigation canal,
cutting up, laughing, wincing
the whole way. What happened to us?

Look, lizard brain; everything we fear
will happen, will happen.
Rivers will rise, dams will burst,
earth will quake, volcanoes will erupt
people will suffer and perish.
Cherry picking bruised, rotting details

doesn't stall entropy.
If you mean to pace what ifs
and heave either/or sighs,
forget it. If you mean to consume
every how-to book for dummies,
you should know, no amount

of information constructs
comfort with ambiguity.
If you mean to master mind reading
and augury, good luck with that.
If you mean to eat and drink
to saturation, here's news:

those escapes are no longer options.
Fretting doesn't tick off the to-do list,
won't add years to dogs' lives.
Stop checking to make sure he's still
breathing. Release
your choke hold.

Stop oughting me.
Stop poisoning me.
Stop shoulding on me!
Unclench your knotted fists;
accept this gift
of letting go.

WYOMING, EARLY SUMMER

Like driving in a blizzard white out,
thick smoke obscures visibility.
Chosen by lightening, three thousand acres
of lodgepole pine burn hot along

Broken Back Creek. Every summer
I revisit this smoke-choked trapezoid
I wonder what it is
I so miss about this place.

Back around 1990,
propelled by newfound singularity,
I skied solo into a charred stand
behind Pahaska Lodge.

A henge of charcoal trunks stood witness,
casualties of the 1988 Clover Mist Blaze
halted just short
of devouring the cabins.

Hell rode in on the wind,
the Cody Enterprise reported.
We could hear the flames,
feel the heat, the owner said.

Freaky, like a painted setting
you might see in a play.
Suddenly, the wind shifted
leaving that hungry flame wall
standing still for the fight.

In one of the spared cabins
I soundly slept that night
among silken black ghosts
voiceless to moan against the wind.

And woke to new snow
sanctifying old killing grounds.
To a gentle bison sleeping
like a windblown drift beneath my window.

Perhaps He Is You

THE GREENER THE DEEPER

There are no beautiful surfaces without a terrible depth.
                                                    Friedrich Nietzsche

Out west, nestled in the Absaroka range's blue summits
sits a true lake. Nearly 8,000 feet above sea level, largest
        high elevation lake in North America.

Enroute, we pass the dam that pools the Shoshone
into a reservoir. From the highway, the reservoir is brown,
        not aqua as I'd imagined. When we arrive,
from every angle, the true lake is opaque as oiled iron.

Until he broke both legs that Christmas Eve,
my father worked away. Until I was twelve, my mother dressed me
        like dolls she wished to own.

Against their unified objections—they never agree—
        I buy the souvenir captain's hat, something a boy would wear.

Empowered by water spray, I skip carefree and careless
        along riprap shoreline. Against swirling wind,
the hat tames my stringy hair that won't hold ringlets.
        One of her greatest disappointments about me.

That year on the cusp, my bones stop reaching, muscles stop layering.
        Girl on verge dressing a woman's body in rags.
Still climbing fences and trees. Feet three sizes bigger than his.
        Taller than her. She can't bring herself to buy me clothes my size.

I have always known the smell of winter and frozen water.
Chill of mountain morning and evening air. And desert heat.
Always both. Aren't we all hybrids of some sort?

Junior High me wanted to swan dive, run laps, shoot hoops,
You're not really athletic. She hisses *athletic* into the air like profanity.
Another hex to ensure a sedentary future.
Without permission, I cut my hair. Short. Blunt.

Before that. Twelfth winter. Fully grown.
Fever dreams from Christmas to February.
Lacing new skates. Slipping. Falling. Rising.
Slipping. Falling. Then skating clumsy jagged slices.

I loved that magical dream place. Burning below the ice.
Watching myself glide all weightless grace atop honed blades.
Still love it there. Though I don't return often.

After the virus, my ox-heavy knee joints ache into spring and onward
Kneeling at the sinner's altar generates obligatory tears.
I practice prayer sitting up, read the King James through. Twice.
Begin to lose faith in beliefs that do not tingle my spine.

Pungent pine sap. Thinner colder air. Not a dream. I was there.
Moss and breeze, skating frozen Black Hills lake water.
Not home, where every bread-heavy meal is a sedative. Where
a clock radio blasting country music invades every dream.

Still love the boy who, like a knight, lifted me from the ice
where I collapsed. Fevered sleep on the ice, a bewitched princess
awaiting the awakening kiss. The boy, not a prince, never kissed me.

Two score later, it was not easy watching my father
owed under that way. Brain swimming in yellow infection. Drowning
    in fungal fever. No hero could pull him back to the surface.

Jot easy watching ice crust along hollow December's ides.
    Breathing sweet Juniper and Sage to find the scents
nerely June memory.

So seldom was it just him and me.
    Out on the boat that day, did I even know?

Rare family vacation. Ice cream bucket full of Grandma's
    raisin cookies. At the tackle shop, I want a keepsake.
t's gaudy. My mother sneers at the bypass twin aquamarine ring.
    I buy it. Anyway. Because. For a dollar. A dollar I earned.

knew nothing of praise or sacrifice. Except they belonged
    to her God who hates jewelry. What I already knew
f absence I would not understand for many seasons.

Sunrise. Sunday. Father's Day. Orange life vests. My captain's hat.
    Morning's first rays skip jeweled light across gentle wave caps.

Ve drift across a palette of botanical greens: algae, pale fern,
    celadon, kelp, to artichoke, and avocado hide.
Rock hypnotically. Not even close to the middle, the lake is so huge.

Trailing my fingers along the icy water's surface, I study
    yellow fire breaking against facets of pale blue glass
ircling my finger. Casting into the black green, my father says,
    Don't drop it over the side. Be lost forever, he warns.

The true lake, a volcanic caldera 390 feet at its depth, 40 degrees cold
  slowly tilts, marshing its southern shore, beaching its northern.
Once I was a sound swimmer. But here even an Olympian could freeze
  to death within twenty minutes.

I peer into lightless depths. Imagine diving.
  Holding my breath till my lungs burn and burst.
Unable to touch bottom as I can at the deep end of the city pool.

  His ambivalence is clear: He will not enter any black-green
icy depth. Not for my one-dollar faux birthstone.
  Which would not gleam down there. Not for me, his firstborn.

  In later years, we sometimes spoke of love's limits.
But never of all the ways we would come to lose beloved things.
  And never of the part of us that remains on that boat.

IDLE HANDS

My mother could knit
until her hands forgot how
to do anything but hold a cigarette.

A woman who sewed wardrobes,
grew and preserved gardens, cooked
and cleaned, and wrote always

reaching for constant gratification.
When my father got sober, addiction
counselors told him to keep busy.

He tore out the front door, built
a chimney and installed a wood burning
stove which provided a purpose

for chopping firewood all winter.
A man who farmed two steads, fed
herds, repaired machinery,

and maintained a 19-year affair
with the other woman, needed more
to do to keep him out of the bar.

Just how much honest work
is enough to prevent us
becoming toys of the gods?

RENEGOTIATION

In that gauzy gray light that subdues
the verdant after-rain blues and greens,
that sometimes suddenly overlays clarity and sound
judgement, whence intrudes this vision of you
dying in the room that kept your parents' secrets.

The first time this scene appears, you are not ill.
This is not daydreaming; it's not at all wishful.
Thirty plus years sober, you shifted course,
the circumstances of your demise less predictable,
less imminent though eventually, like everyone's,

certain. You liked to joke about others' ends,
and especially your own: *We all start dying*
the minute we're born, you'd chuckle
at every funeral. We suspect your ex-wife
slash platonic roommate will poison you

or now, blood pressure high, blind like Odin
in the left eye, a likely stroke (some hope, some pray
it takes you quickly and completely).
But that's not how it goes. I don't need to recount
all the ways we failed each other.

This is old ground we will dwell upon
as long as either of us remains, perhaps
beyond, common ground, so many before
seem to have spoken every possible metaphor.
I don't worry about some misstep.

I know when to leave a room,
when to stay away, when I'm too much.
Don't worry; I remember you
for more than faults, more than betrayal,
more than an unheroic death.

Years before, I saw us (more than once)
in this future moment. I am not there
to blame or comfort or forgive.
I am just there. Drowning in infection
you hold on until I can drive from Missouri

to Montana in December.
You wait for me to sit beside you,
take your hand,
so much your mother's hand,
and say, *Next time, I get to be the dad.*

Your gnarled index finger twitches,
points from your chest to the ceiling,
an echo
of your one-fingered farmer wave
lifting off the steering wheel.

THE FIRST LAW

of thermodynamics states
Energy is
neither created nor destroyed,
only transformed.

Probably I misunderstand, as I do most
science, this fundamental concept.
It seems to come down
to what we can learn from absence:

How those fallen leaves decay
enriching the soil, feeding the roots
of the tree that unfurls new buds;
how that maverick river crashes down

with such force, a potential energy
harnessed & spun like wool from turbine
to generator to alternating current
to flow through filaments into light;

how the very air drinks of the river
& my skin to form fat heavy clouds
of steam & rain & sleet, liquid
to vapor to solid to liquid to vapor,

an enduring cycle. It might seem
that tree once felled, split, burned,
its dense matter consumed by flame,
released as heat, no longer exists.

Yet its ash remains
nourishing soil pounded from stones.
These alterations determine
death is not a condition

but an event between states:

The brief flame between wood & ash
the heat of which is grief.
An evaporation between cloud & rain
a quiet space to examine the soul.

A violent churning from river to current
an engine to carry us forward to metamorphosis.

LOST LAST WORDS

The last time
I spoke to my father alive I told him
don't worry about Christmas
cookies and fudge; I'll take care of it.

At least a decade before I'd begun
to regift the plastic containers of crumbles
and sugary overcooked Penuchi
that traced us around the country to my sons.

In his last cognizant exchange with anyone
he said *well, if nothing else . . .*
and mumbled an incoherent instruction
or request or deluded observation.

For all I will never know
it may have been his funniest joke ever.
Though not an apology; he never breathed
words that could be mistaken for *I'm sorry.*

LUCKY IN DREAMS

Before pinkish dawn
my distorted reflection floats
upon the shimmer of fuchsia
and aqua bulbs loosely dangled
on tinseled Lodgepole pine branches.

Whatever happened
to those elegant ornaments—
blown glass onion domes,
snow-crested turrets,
salt-crystal snowflakes, (never
an infant savior in a manger)—
raiment for the Charlie Brown
trees you dragged in year after year?

Kept so carelessly paper wrapped
in that musty water-weathered
cardboard box beneath the sink
in the utility room,
who wrested, on fair grounds,
ownership of the keepsakes?
Whoever cradles them now?

They were not in your collection
of ghosts from an insane past,
cartons of memory remnants
rescued from a shattered
home. I am unable to trace
their whereabouts. Are they all
broken, too? Did they depart
with her, along with the gold
tasseled cords tying back brocade
drapes too heavy, too stiff to soften
against even Wyoming wind?

Across waves pulsing
inside dark night my sister speaks
of a woman's voice that reassures her.
Not an internal voice; a clear resonance
from outside, like bamboo chimes.

The voice of my comforter is male,
sonorous, soothing as old vine zinfandel.
Someone says *candle* and I hear *gamble*,
hear *grudge* for *trudge*. We prowl
warily through this season.

The children still reminisce about you,
driving the mower, riding the ditch,
the homemade cookies and fudge.

I still slip through the open neck
into the silver globe of my underworld
to dream of lacing tight
new white leather skates.
I stumble across
the canal's thick, rough ice,
my forward toe-picking footwork
chips a trail of crow's feet
to follow backward.

I duck through culverts, glide
beneath abandoned trestles
until dusk oozes gray
into the cracks of bluest coldest
December sky crazed as old
porcelain; I cry icicles, scared
I will never return home.

Again I wake and rise
into the silent void of absence,
into the no longer waiting
for packages that won't arrive,
with no heirlooms to hang,
no sacred trust to tumble
from my weakening grip
hurling its fragile temporality
against the rising floor.

Anyway, I've lost the appetite
to scarf down sweets
that sand my tongue raw.

The only present we desire
is your presence.

PERHAPS HE IS YOU

Black chia seeds engorged
with vanilla protein drink
deliver the saccharine aftertaste
of artificial sweetener, an experiment
I likely won't replicate.

Yesterday the salad Romaine
and cabbage soup carried an acerbic
edge, the metallic potassium chloride
of salt substitute and swallowed tears.
An aluminum tang some claim can't be

tasted, but is a machination of imagin-
ation bent on excuses. The bitterness
matched the ice-needled storm slashing
gray air at acute angles, wedging and
widening from an unseen vertex above.

Consciousness surfaced unbidden
at 3:00 a.m. or perhaps arrived to rescue
a dreamer from confusions of reservations
and impossible logistics, from frustration,
a natural byproduct of losing control.

Today seems an important layer.
It is a myth that fingernails and hair,
which require blood flow, which requires
oxygen, continue to grow postmortem.
Those who've seen mistook the cuticle

shrinking back from nail beds and flesh
from scalp and around the mouth pulling
lips away from teeth, mummifying
like a drying apple doll, as a continuance.
Perhaps to prolong the inevitable process

is preferable to life's final ruling. Perhaps
the boy in the dream waving
from the other side of the tracks is not my son.
The boy who can't cross the stubbled field,
the boy who can't come near hard as he tries.

HOW WE IMAGINE THE FIRE

Tell the children he drifted
loose in a warm room, dreamt
himself to a mound of satiny ash.

Tell them the dead don't feel
anything anymore. In the retort
a body doesn't burn like the trunk

of lightening-struck cottonwood
smoldering orange coals for days.
Doesn't start to a pugilistic stance

like a prize fighter, fists cocked
to bloody a nose. We are more like
Styrofoam: flesh shrinks back

from bone; fat melts, drips, hisses
feeding the flames; muscle sears
like thick steaks on a grill

left too long, overdone, blackened
to char; a skull may shatter
but not explode. There's a difference

I guess. Wait: Tell them
he was a kite, a diamond frame
of balsa overlain with yesterday's

news and obituaries, a tail
of cotton twine and rag bows.
Tangled among treetops

for so long, that same cradle-
rocking wind at last swept him
to the sun, his penultimate goal.

A FORGIVENESS

Three alfalfa cuttings baled, stacked, awaiting need.
Field-dried corn chopped, wet packed, fermenting to feed.
A good year. Just two silos per farm. Grain, beans,

all overflow when prices in town are too low
to see us through winter. While waiting an increase,
hire idle lads to tighten barbed wire to fence domestic herds

to fatten in fallow fields on the detritus of harvest,
on hay scattered cold snowy mornings from the flatbed,
on mangers filled with heady silage slurped clean daily.

Grateful our forebears abandoned the barbarisms of trapping
generations ago, from here to May it's all husbandry.
We'll pay more to feed livestock than ourselves.

The women salvage every seed, preserve every vegetable,
fruit, and legume coaxed from this arid plain. The men
trench soil, burn weeds, irrigate from ditches

they know like Catechism. Better than their own veins.
Even in twilight their eyes sting from long days bent
beneath the sun they serve, skin they expose

nine shades redder. They sleep in sweat and worry,
smell diesel, hear engines grind, blades thresh, hydraulics
of labor they grease and oil and repair and pamper along.

The weathervane spins, a wild roulette determining
fortunes bet on elements, fret over rain, drought, blight,
frost, pestilence. There will be no fortunes.

The best scenario is survival. Each morn
to four directions we turn admiring stone cathedrals ringing
the lands awaiting first light cresting late above peaks

and later each day as indoors rooms glow large
of rising dough and steaming stoves and firelight.
Each room a hearth within a home, a world inside

a world where we remember ourselves beyond work.
All but the most robust of birds take leave for a season.
We wish them well, hold no grudges. Those who leave

will return changed. Meanwhile, we weather here
where pines are faithful, stars stable. Too worn to remember
struggle, nothing more to do for now but remain stoic.

Ditch Rider

PILGRIMAGE: I-90 WEST

1
A landmark, this dead cottonwood's
weathered gray bark long ago
shelled away as secrets laid bare,
as armor lain down,
reincarnated now, a bleached bone
wrist jutting up from underworld,
open palm praising sky,
branched fingers ringed
with dozens of red-winged blackbirds.

2
Rushing westward
alongside bloated wetland
hot glassy blacktop keens
like the rim of leaded crystal,
rumble strip drums a pulse,
bordering lush green marsh
barrow ditch grasses sway,
and beyond scythed dusty sage acres
sun dry, await shaping to bales.

3
Paired Mallards bob buoyant
and flapless as decoys.
The waterline rises
as if displaced by all those ducks.
Pawns of a stiff wind,
cattail fronds fan ripples
roadward urging sodden soil:
More. More. Last chance
to swallow more.

4

Badlands, bear country, Sioux country.
Abandoned clapboard pioneer homesteads,
frontier ghost towns, antique malls, and tractor
museums house artifacts of an obsolete past.
Cottonwood groves have stood a century
watching, listening, showing the way to water.
Such hard beauty demands stolid character.
In his ingenuity, even L. Frank Baum couldn't
make Aberdeen work when the heartland eroded to
silt.

5

Set against crystal Olympic blue,
from flat planes white steel giants rise
erect and all business. Modern shapes
of an ancient magic methodically
churn wind to voltage, feed the beast.
Nemesis of iron rigs run by wooden men.
Threat to the heavy dredging
machinery displacing mountains
ripping into earth's coal seams.

6

Burly dry clouds drift like ghost bison
over Thunder Basin grasslands.
The buffalo here no more, their medicine
hangs heavy on the big wind.

7
A Lakota woman named Wynona
had a vision for this place:
Buffalo and *windmills*, she pressed
her words like a token into my palm.
Buffalo and *windmills*
as far as the eye can see.
Out here where the Brown & Gold asserts
The World Needs More Cowboys
the Blue & White responds *The World Needs More Saints.*

CAROUSEL

They couldn't tell us anything back then.

From cocoons of solitude
into elaborate costumes of adulthood
we emerge, something larval still
calling forth, pulling from behind

as reimagined and reinvented we
retrace the streets and avenues we paced—
on foot, on two wheels, in trucks and muscle
cars—in square circles cross-wiring

the grid layout, the back-to-back block
structures of turn-of-century brick
buildings, the local businesses
occupying, producing, serving,

pumping life through a desert
settlement sprung from diverted waters.
The optometrist's office is now a favorite
Mexican restaurant, J.C. Penney's a Habitat

thrift shop, the five & dime drugstore fountain
where my mother concocted floats
now a museum relic. The bakery of four
decades no longer perfumes the main drag

with sweet breads and soup, no longer bakes
signature secret recipe cream-filled long johns.
Evolution seems cruel: into this place where
we knew everyone, so many unfamiliar

nameless faces fluxed in from afar
stroll our first-home sidewalks where
we rode bikes, newbies eating sub-par pastry
from second-rate chain grocer bakeries.

A steepled church, a post office, precious
names chiseled onto tombstones at Crown Hill,
a flushed pheasant's squabble, a meadowlark's trill,
the touchstones that ground remain.

Disoriented pigeons buffeted by storms,
we return one by one in the shadow
of prophecies of change. No one looks
the same anymore, and nothing gold stays.

We parrot the words our forebears
sighed as omen, as curse,
seeing the new progress
through their old fears.

EVERY FATHER'S DAY

My father passed after a terrifying three-month
battle with a mysterious illness.

We predicted stroke would take him,
not some dust-born fungal infection.

Just like him to die of an obscure
difficult to diagnose and treat disease.

Our relationship was complex,
the stuff of Greek Mythology.

I'm not even sure where to begin:
where Agamemnon barters to appease Artemis

and tricks his oldest daughter Iphigenia
to sacrifice for smooth sailing?

Or the version where the daughter survives
as he returns from the wars with his mistress

Cassandra in tow. He was my subject.
Most photos of him, I snapped.

How starkly those images
isolate raw emotions, something I knew

in a sensory way the lens would capture
which is why I always pointed my camera at him.

The only way I could steal genuine pieces of him
for myself, the only way to pull him close to me

to record for study the tangled knot
of us, of who we were then,

who we are now that it is only me.
In the abiding ache of his absence,

I find comfort that the stolen pieces of his soul
he left behind invite me to laugh as he laughed

at misfortunes, so that when I reminisce
I feel more joy than sorrow.

DITCH RIDER

From wild heady boyhood beyond seasoned
manhood, fifty searing summers he traded Justin Bucks
for knee-high army-green rubber *galoshes* (he joked),
shimmied hips through barbed wire, waded
thigh-high Canadian thistle and knapweed
and every six feet along arid ditch banks
like an altar boy, my father genuflected
right knee braced against gray silt, hands suctioning
s-shaped aluminum tubes syphoning liquid gold
to serve each corrugate in every rocky field.
Playing mortal god mixing mud to reshape
a high desert into an iota of the Miocene Eden
it once was. Between irrigations, he teetered
atop a barstool in town sipping Seagram's 7

awaiting his water ration as crops wilted.
Bread and flesh, blood and water, people steal
what they need for survival. Daily over lunch
he dropped names of farmers caught opening head-
gates. And one high noon a visit from district
flushed out his own confession of guilt.
After failing the farm, my father landed
on the other side of the canal policing flow.
They say the best detectives are reformed
criminals. Or maybe he was more of a defector
turned spy, a double agent who knew how
the enemy operates. So he became in his liberty
and sobriety an old man seeking heaven,
a steward of honesty. Sheriff of waiting turns.

BRIDGE

Attempts to repair ruptured trusts
have been hit or miss. Since Thursday
brought no good news.

While a floral future stirs and stretches
below ground, from high up a ceramic
bluebird suffers imposter syndrome.

If we could go back, even a week,
scrub the ego nonsense from the script,
gather around mutual beating hearts,

if we could savor authentic embraces,
perhaps save enough time
to pay ourselves back what's wasted

rather than berating those comatose
from loss who could not attend
to the same old tired sermon,

we might understand how car hours
pass slower in silence, how returning
to a house where every timepiece

is set back an hour and two weeks
proves time can't jump ahead
without our manipulation.

Telling every living body who came
how we tried to organize that storm
brought no peace.

Though paging through the gravedigger's
handwritten ledger of the local dead
tells a story of dates, and sums, and plots.

Walking the granite rows, we see
even some of those stones worn
and weathered. What chance have we?

South of Crown Hill, Dry Lake rests,
the same alkaline patch of inarable
earth as when our family existed.

Everyone who isn't ready leaves
a mess. It's a drag to think about.
What's a good word to end on?

ADULARESCENCE

What can mend the ravenous beetles'
work in satisfying its violent hunger?
Iridescent ovals, coppery green shimmers
munch vacancies, render violet-
veined petals to eyelet, so that
sunlight drips through each teardrop bite.

Spring fires streak opalescent pink-gold,
shroud peaks in charcoal gray smoke.
Sandwiched between infrared and ultraviolet
rays, we lose the visible blue green labradorite
play scattering schillers from deep clefts.
We imagine they travel south robed in clouds.

On such a day, let us submit to soft pearlescent
selenite said to be self-cleansing. Dedicate
this day to repairing the rent. Begin to notice
our second-hand hearts in a whole new way.
Attend to the blood's rhythm, dispel myths
of damage as a life sentence.

Stop rubbing saline drops that sting our eyes.
Clean stones are rare.
Beauty sings out
from internal fractures dispersing
refracted light into rainbows,
scars carved by deprivation.

SRI YANTRA

Laying down a thick coat of rich waxy color
on the large abstract Mandela, as with everything, I begin
from the outer border rather than the center. Beyond,

churning peripheral sunlight into geometry
through the wavy antique glass, rustling leaves whisper
my father's mantra: *When will you learn to pay attention?*

Past my fence, across the street, inside their fence,
the neighbors' lawn full of dry gold glistens and chatters
in the breeze. Hazy from this distance, I put on my bifocals.

I always see their yard more clearly. Still shimmering
pliant and green, my Cottonwoods' leaves will turn last,
a dangerous delay fooling me into believing

there is always tomorrow to wash these windows.
In the frenetic leaving and coming and leaving,
laundry, dishes, bills, dust piles up—all going nowhere—

as if there is a forever right here. I know better. I spent
the morning in direct sunlight scrubbing forty years
of cigarette tar off Granny's white Hoosier cabinet.

There is no end to the negligence I could confess.
Mostly I have been careless with time and love and money
as if there is always more. Some would say I keep to myself

too often, my mind seldom present. I won't deny it.
This morning a multi-faceted ruby caught in the center
of a dream web spun me into this waking, my first thought

always of lost loves. Today there was desire here to care
for my little world. I move into the Mandela and color the center
diamond ruby. Everything today happened right inside this poem.

I WAS TRYING TO SAY

that hunger is not sin;
exhaustion is not immoral.
Food was comfort, sleep often sanctuary.
But there was never waking without fear.
That if Abraham had not traded Haggar
for Sarah, Ishmael for Isaac, or
even before if Adam had not favored
one son's offering above the other's
they could have spared the world
this much war. Or, that if we quit
believing those ancient even fictional
rejections still matter—now
there's something to consider.
That unlike romance languages
(the French you forbade at the table)
English has no reflexive verbs, per se; so
to betray can be transitive and intransitive.
That only the trusted can lead us astray, let
our secrets slip; that we are most complicit
in delivering ourselves to foes
as only those we love can truly wound us.
Jesus knew this; you taught me this.
That winters in Wyoming are long, but the rain
in Missouri is more disheartening than snow.
That every single convoluted metaphor
is a pathetic disguise for need. That there
was sometimes beauty but never grace.
That longing and desire and passion
are all distorted faces of the same trail boss
who rides herd over our motives.
That at times, rejection delivered vile threats.
We are sorry about that.
That not all the actors drank whiskey
or smoked Marlboros like the cowboy
they portrayed. One didn't even like horses
but rode them anyway. Not everyone is in love
with the masculine or the equine. That it's perfectly
reasonable to be ambivalent that way.

IN WHICH A THERAPIST HELPS ME UNDERSTAND NOT EVERY FAMILY WAS LIKE MINE

What if we stack atop unmarked ash
scattered across sandy soils where overturned
sedimentary rocks smoothed by ages
ruined his plow blades, a cairn of bone China,
fill the saucers with pearls, adorn it with moss.

What if we thread strands of last century's
superstitions—yeah, yeah—wind them
like webs about old clock works fastened
inside a shadow box until a monstrous Eye
of God bristles like a purple aster.

What if we polish to luster the effortless
daily disasters, his talent to fleece
women of honor, smooth as bourbon, precise
as his form when he threw that loop to lasso
a calf, no effort for a cowboy's cowboy.
What if I just don't clot your memory

with my stories of disoriented drunks
who froze in blizzards, or how there would
never be a proper swimming pool for kids.
How we'll all drown swallowing a language
with only one word for stone, in which stone
carries a hundred different meanings.

What if I tell you instead how the Blue Jay
escaped the cat's jaws, circled the open rooms
searching for sanctuary, how flapping to be sure
she could still fly, found an opening
of crystal sky and swooped through the door jamb
like one breathy note from a wooden flute.

About the Author

Shelly Norris resides on the Montana Hi Line where she teaches Liberal Arts and Communications at Aaniiih Nakoda College on the Fort Belknap Reservation. Her poems and short fiction have appeared in a variety of publications. Her first collection titled *Hyperbola* debuted February 2024.

Acknowledgements

Dry Lake
appeared July 2021 in Volume 8, Number 7 of Verse-Virtual

Marlboro Man
appeared July 13, 2022 in Rye Whiskey Review

An Embarrassment of Wild Prairie Roses
appeared July 14, 2024 in Journal of Expressive Writing

Elegy on Pugsley
appeared September, 2022 in Zooanthology by Sweety Cat Press

Waking Raw
appeared November 30, 2020 in Spillwords Press

Some Mornings
appeared March 21, 2020 in The Writer's Club

Puce
appeared July 28, 2021 in Spillwords Press

I Will Not Sing at the Funeral
appeared February 1, 2022 in the print anthology Songs of Life by Sweety Cat Press

How We Imagine the Fire
appeared September 2023 in VOL 10 NO 9 of Verse-Virtual

Ditch Rider
appeared June 1, 2022 in the print anthology Movement: Our Bodies in Action by Sweety Cat Press

Confessions of a Solar Daughter
appeared in 2012 in Issue II of Open Window Review

Adularescence
appeared September 2, 2025 in Amethyst Review

Sri Yantra
appeared April 11, 2020 in Academy of the Heart and Mind

I Was Trying to Say
appeared March 23, 2023 in Spillwords Press

In Which a Therapist Helps Me Understand Not Every Family Was Like Mine
appeared April 1, 2024 in Issue 24 of Gyroscope Review

I Inherit Vitrine
appeared November 2025 in The Haiku Shack

Unmoored, Grief Jumble, and Perhaps He Is You
appeared October 2025 in Volume 12, Number 1 of Verse-Virtual

Powder River Publishing

www.powderriverpublishing.com